Hearty Soups That'll Your Soul

PUBLISHED BY LAWRENCE FARBER

@ Marco Perry

Soups: Hearty Soups That'll Your Soul

ISBN 978-87-975096-1-6

TABLE OF CONTENTS

Oxtail Soup

Ingredients:

- Olive oil

- 125 ml of red wine

- 3 tins of chopped tomatoes

- 2 carton of tomato juice

- Good squeeze of tomato purée

- 500g/1lb of button mushrooms

- A few bay leaves

- Salt and pepper

- 1 cup of chopped onion

- 1 cup of leek

- 1 cup of carrot

- 1 cup of celery

- 1kg/2 ¼ lbs of fresh tomatoes

- A couple of onions

- Fresh rosemary, thyme and basil

- 1.5kg/3 lbs oxtail

- 3 cups of any other mixed vegetables

- 100g /4ozs sobrasada (optional)

- 100g/4ozs of chopped chorizo

- A teaspoon of paprika

- A teaspoon of molasses sugar

- A teaspoon of balsamic vinegar

Directions:

1. Firstly, start with 1kg of fresh tomatoes (home grown if possible).. Chop a couple of onions and add to a large pan, with some fresh rosemary, thyme and basil, along with a good pinch of salt and half a pint of water. Bring to the boil and then simmer for 1 hour. Mash down with a masher to make sure all the juices are released.

2. Season your Oxtail by putting a spoon of plain flour, salt and pepper in a plastic shopping (2 with holes). Hold top together and shake to mix then add your Oxtail pieces and shake again. A peek inside should reveal your beautifully and evenly coated and seas2d oxtail. So, in another pressure cooker sized saucepan, fry off around 1.5kg of seas2d Oxtail in some olive oil (or the fat skimmed off another soup). Brown all over and then add to

a slow cooker along with the strained (and rubbed through a sieve) tomatoes.

3. After tipping away the fat from the pan you used to brown the Oxtail in, add a good glug of red wine to the bottom of the Oxtail pan and de-glaze (or scrape wIth fury) the burnt bits off the bottom of the pan. Then add 3 tins of chopped tomatoes and 2 carton of tomato juice. Wash out each container with some water and a good shake and add to the pan, along with a very good squeeze of tomato purée. Bring to the boil and add that mix to the slow cooker along with 1lb of button mushrooms, and some fresh rosemary and thyme and a few bay leaves. Add a good pinch of salt and pepper.

4. Add some chopped onion, leek, carrot and celery, along with any other mixed vegetables you have to hand. (I used frozen peas and

beans and a bag of cauliflower, carrot and broccoli, courgette and onion that I picked up in a 'bargain bucket', but use anything you have to hand.

5. Sobrasada, the Mallorcan sausage, also makes a good addition.

6. Add 100g of chopped chorizo, a teaspoon of paprika, molasses sugar and balsamic vinegar. Taste and adjust seasoning (this dish can handle a lot of salt)

7. Leave to cook for 7 hours (make in the morning, eat when you get home) on a high (slow cooker setting, very low if stove top).

8. At the end of cooking, skim off all the fat and store in a jar in the fridge (it's too good to waste). Taste and adjust the seasoning. Now, you have a couple of choices to make: 2, with vegetables or without. Because of the length of cooking time, most of the vegetables in the

soup will be mostly mush. If you don't want to serve these then strain the soup through a colander and then just serve the rich tomato soupy sauce. Your second choice relates to the Oxtail itself. You can serve it on or off the b2. Obviously, on the b2 Is going to be a delightfully messy affair, with your diners probably picking up the oxtail and gnawing dog like, so if you're looking to impress the bank manager or new boss, then that might not be the best option. If that's the case, then remove b2s from soup and scrape off meat and return that to the pan, with or without the vegetables. For the record, I served mine on the b2, with just the saved mushrooms (and obviously, the yummy Oxtail soup)

Spicy Lentil Chili With Beans

Ingredients:

- 1 ½ cups water

- can fire roasted chopped tomatoes

- f2 ½ cups cooked lentils brown or green

- 1 ½ cups black beans drained and rinsed

- 1 ½ cups pinto beans drained and rinsed

- ½ teaspoon st2ground mustard

- 1 teaspoon hot sauce optional

- ½ teaspoon salt or to taste

- ½ teaspoon organic canola oil

- ½ medium yellow onion chopped

- 2 cloves garlic minced

- 2 teaspoons coriander

- f2 teaspoons cumin

- 2 teaspoons ancho chili powder

Directions:

1. Bring a soup pot to a medium heat with oil. Saute onion and garlic for a few minutes, until translucent and fragrant.

2. Add coriander, cumin, and ancho chili powder to pot. Saute with onions and garlic for about 30 seconds.

3. Then add the following to the soup pot: water, fire roasted chopped tomatoes, lentils, black beans, pinto beans, mustard, hot sauce , and salt.

4. Bring the chili to a simmer. Cook for fifteen minutes, allowing the flavors to meld and the chili to thicken.

5. Optional: After the chili has thickened, use an immersion blender in the soup pot for 3 or 4 seconds to break up some of the tomatoes and beans. It also thickens the soup further.

6. You don't want to blend the chili completely. It should still be chunky.

7. However, a few seconds with the immersion blender gives some added texture and thickens the chili even more. After blending, allow the chili to cook for a few more minutes.

8. Ladle the chili into bowls. Serve with crackers or tortilla chips, if you like.

Curry Lentil Soup

Ingredients:

- 1 cup dried red lentils rinsed

- 2 ½ cups water

- 1 teaspoon curry powder + more if desired

- ¼ teaspoon cumin

- ½ teaspoon coriander

- Generous pinch salt

- 1 teaspoon extra virgin olive oil or any neutral flavored oil

- ½ onion chopped small

- 2 cloves garlic minced

- Chopped cilantro optional garnish

Directions:

1. Bring a soup pot to a medium heat with extra virgin olive oil.
2. Add onion and garlic to the pot and sauté for a few minutes, until they are softened and fragrant. Then add the remaining Ingredients: to the pot.
3. Bring the soup to a simmer. Then turn the heat to low and cover for 15 to 20 minutes, stopping occasionally to stir.
4. Once the lentils have softened and are starting to break down while still maintaining some of their shape, the soup is ready.
5. Taste for more curry powder and salt, if necessary. Ladle the soup into bowls and top with cilantro garnish

Udon Noodle Soup With Miso Tahini Broth

Ingredients:

- 2 cups water

- 1 teaspoon Better Than Bouillon, no chicken base or your preferred vegetable bouillon

- 2 teaspoons white miso paste

- 1 Tablespoon tamari

- ½ teaspoon sriracha

- 2 Tablespoons tahini

- 3.5 ounces baked tofu or super firm tofu, cut into cubes

- Big handful baby spinach divided

- 250 gram pouch frozen udon noodles Or 1 cup cooked noodles of your choice.

- ½ teaspoon organic canola oil or other neutral flavored oil

- ½ onion chopped

- 2 cloves garlic minced

- ¼ to ½ teaspoon sesame oil divided, optional garnish

Directions:

1. Start by cooking frozen udon noodles according to package Directions:, then draining the noodles.

2. If you aren't using frozen udon noodles, cook your preferred type of noodle. You will need 1 cooked cup of pasta in total.

3. While the noodles are cooking, bring a soup pot to a medium heat with oil. Saute onions and garlic until translucent and fragrant. This will take a few minutes

4. Add water, Better Than Bouillon no chicken base, miso paste, tamari, sriracha, and tahini to the pot.

5. Stir until everything is evenly combined. You want the miso paste and tahini to dissolve into the broth.

6. Add cubed tofu and a big handful of baby spinach to the tahini broth. Allow the spinach to wilt in the soup.

7. Put 2 half of the drained noodles in a soup bowl and 2 half in the other bowl. Top the

noodles with miso tahini broth, spinach, and tofu.

8. Finish the bowls of soup with a drizzle of sesame oil. It's optional, but it really brings out the "sesame-ness" of the tahini. Not too much sesame oil is needed.

9. About ⅛ to ¼ teaspoon of sesame oil per bowl is plenty.

Moi Peanut Soup

Ingredients:

- 3 tablespoons flour

- 1 tablespoon finely chopped lemongrass

- 1 teaspoon chopped red chile

- 14 ounces chicken broth

- 1 1/2 cups unsweetened coconut milk

- 1/2 cup peanut butter

- 1/3 cup onion(chopped)

- 1/3 cup celery(chopped)

- 1/3 cup carrot(chopped)

- 3 tablespoons sweet red peppers(chopped)

- 1 tablespoon butter

- 2 tablespoons soy sauce

Directions:

1. Cook onion, celery, carrot and red pepper in butter until softened, about 5 minutes.
2. Add the lemon grass, red chili, stir and cook for 1 minute. Stir in the flour, and let cook for 1 minute, stirring all the time.
3. Add chicken broth, coconut milk and soy sauce, and stir to combine well. Add the peanut butter. Keep stirring until well combined. Heat until hot and bubbly.
4. Serve with chopped fresh roasted peanuts and green onions as a garnish.

Zucchini Soup

Ingredients:

- 2 cloves garlic (sliced)

- 4 cups chicken stock

- 2 tbsp. coconut milk

- 3 medium zucchinis on skin (cut it into large size chunks)

- 1 onion (quartered)

- Paleo cooking fat

- Sea salt & ground black pepper

Directions:

1. Melt some cooking fat in a saucepan placed over a medium heat.

2. Add the onion, garlic and zucchinis and cook
    for 4 to 5 minutes.

3. Add the chicken stock, season to taste with
    salt and pepper, and bring to a boil.

4. Lower the heat, cover, and let simmer until
    the zucchinis are tender, about 20 minutes.

5. Remove from the heat, add the coconut milk,
    and purée with an immersion blender

6. Adjust the seasoning and serve hot.

Kidney Soup

Ingredients:

- 2 tbsp lemon juice

- 10 whole black peppercorns

- 2 large sprigs thyme

- 1 bay leaf

- 8 cups beef

- 2 tbsp cooking fat

- 1 1/2 lbs lamb kidneys

- 2 onions(coarsely chopped)

- 2 carrots (sliced)

- Sea salt and ground black pepper

Directions:

1. Prepare the kidneys by removing any membrane covering them, if present.
2. Cut them in half lengthwise and cut around the fatty white core to remove it. Cut each kidney half into thick slices.
3. Heat a stockpot over a medium heat, add the cooking fat and cook the onions, stirring occasionally, until they start to soften, about 6 minutes.
4. Add the kidney slices to the hot pot and brown them on each side.
5. Pour in the stock and add the whole peppercorns, thyme sprigs and bay leaf.
6. Bring to a boil, then reduce to a simmer and let simmer, covered, for about 3 hours.
7. Add the carrot slices in the last 45 minutes of cooking.

8. When the soup is ready, discard the thyme sprigs and the bay leaf, and use a slotted spoon to remove most of the whole peppercorns.

Mystyle Soup

Ingredients:

- 1 bottle 341 ml local lager

- 15 ml Dijon mustard

- 1 litre chicken broth

- 6 thick slices baguette (toasted)

- 500 ml cheddar cheese(grated)

- 2.5 litres thinly sliced onions

- 60 ml butter

- 15 ml flour

- Salt and pepper

Directions:

1. In a large non-stick saucepan, sauté the onions in the butter over medium to low heat until lightly browned and tender, about 30 minutes.
2. Season with salt and pepper. Sprinkle the onions with the flour and cook for 1 minute.
3. Add the beer and mustard and bring to a boil while stirring. Add the broth and bring to a boil. Simmer for about 10 minutes. Add chicken broth, if needed. Adjust the seasoning.
4. With the rack in the middle position, preheat the oven's broiler.
5. Ladle the soup into four heat resistant bowls. Place a slice of bread on each soup and cover with the cheese.
6. Place the bowls on a baking sheet and broil in the oven until the cheese has melted.

Cold Almond & Garlic Soup

Ingredients:

Soup

- 4 cups chicken broth

- 2 cups cubed white bread

- 1 cup sliced almonds

- 6 cloves garlic (chopped)

- 2 tbsp olive oil

- Salt and pepper

Toppings

- 3/4 cup diced white bread

- 2 tbsp olive oil

- 12 seedless green grapes(halved)

Directions:

Soup

1. In a saucepan, brown the almonds and garlic in the oil. Add the broth and bread. Season with salt and pepper. Bring to a boil. Cover and simmer over medium heat for 10 minutes.
2. In a blender, purée the soup for about 5 minutes. Strain through a sieve. Refrigerate until completely chilled.

Topping

3. In a skillet, brown the diced bread in the oil. Season with salt and pepper.
4. Pour the chilled soup into bowls. Garnish with green grapes and bread cubes. Drizzle with olive oil.

Carrot & Coriander Soup

Ingredients:

- 1 tsp ground coriander

- 1 potato, chopped

- 450g carrots, peeled and chopped

- 1.2l vegetable or chicken stock

- 1 tbsp vegetable oil

- 1 onion, chopped

- Handful coriander (about ½ a supermarket packet)

Directions:

1. Heat 1 tbsp vegetable oil in a large pan, add 1 chopped onion, then fry for five mins till softened.
2. Stir in 1 tsp ground coriander and 1 chopped potato, then cook for 1 min.
3. Add the 450g peeled and chopped carrots and 1.2l vegetable or chicken stock, bring to the boil, then reduce the heat.
4. Cover and cook for 20 minutes until the carrots are tender.
5. Tip into a food processor with a handful of coriander then blitz till smooth (you can need to do this in two batches). Return to pan, taste, add salt if necessary, then reheat to serve.

Leek, Bacon & Potato Soup

Ingredients:

- 1 onion, chopped

- 400g pack trimmed leek, sliced and well washed

- 3 medium potatoes, peeled and diced

- 1.4l hot vegetable stock

- 142ml pot single cream

- 25g butter

- 3 rashers streaky bacon, chopped

- 4 rashers streaky bacon, to serve

Directions:

1. Melt the butter in a huge pan, then fry the bacon and onion, stirring till they begin to flip golden.

2. Tip in the leeks and potatoes, stir well, then cover and flip down the heat. Cook gently for five mins, shaking the pan each now and then to make sure that the combination doesn`t catch.

3. Pour in the stock, season well and bring to the boil. Cover and simmer for 20 mins until the vegetables are soft.

4. Leave to cool for a few mins, then blend in a food processor in batches till smooth.

5. Return to the pan, pour in the cream and stir well. Taste and season if necessary.

6. Serve scattered with tasty crisp bacon and devour with toasted or warm crusty bread on the side.

Creamy Fish & Mussel Soup

Ingredients:

- 1l strong, hot fish stock (we used knorr touch of taste concentrate)

- 500g floury potato , cut into sugarcube-size pieces

- 200g mixed fish

- 500g pack mussel in creamy sauce (find these in the chilled aisle)

- Small bunch flatleaf parsley

Directions:

1. Drain the sauce from the mussels into a large saucepan and upload the stock. Tip in the potatoes, cowl and bring to the boil.

2. Once boiling, take off the lid and simmer for about 12 mins or until the potatoes are very tender.

3. Meanwhile, cut the fish into large chunks and roughly chop the parsley.

4. Stir the fish and mussels into the soup, then bring back to a simmer for about three minutes or until the fish has modified colour and flakes easily.

5. Stir in most of the parsley, then serve scattered with the rest of the parsley and eat with crusty bread

Lentil And Black Bean Soup

Ingredients:

- 1 teaspoon chili powder

- 1 cup red lentils

- 1-14.5 ounce can diced tomatoes

- 2 carrots, peeled and finely diced

- 2 cloves garlic, minced

- 1-15 ounce can black beans, drained and rinsed

- 1 tablespoon extra-virgin olive oil

- 4 cups vegetable broth

- ½ teaspoon crushed red pepper flakes

- ½ teaspoon kosher or sea salt

- ½ teaspoon black pepper

- ½ teaspoon cumin

- 1 yellow onion, diced

Directions:

1. Add olive oil into a large pot and sauté garlic for a minute.
2. Add carrots and onions and continue to sauté until the onions are tender. Add the remaining Ingredients:, stir, and cover.
3. Bring to a boil over medium heat, reduce the heat to a simmer, and cook until the lentils and carrots are tender.

Vegetable Soup

Ingredients:

- 1 teaspoon allspice

- ½ teaspoon black pepper

- Pinch of kosher or sea salt

- 1 clove garlic, minced

- 1 small yellow onion, diced

- 1 medium sweet potato, peeled and cut into 1 inch cubes

- 1 stalk celery, diced

- 3 carrots, peeled and sliced

- 4 cups loosely packed baby spinach

- 1 tablespoon plus 1 teaspoon extra-virgin olive oil

- 1-14.5 oz. can diced tomatoes

- 2-15 ounce cans navy beans, drained and rinsed

- 1 bay leaf

- 1 teaspoon paprika

- 4 cups low-sodium vegetable broth

Directions:

1. Add all the Ingredients: to a slow cooker except olive oil and spinach. Cover and cook on low for 6-8 hours.
2. Stir in spinach and continue cooking until it wilts.
3. Drizzle a little olive oil over each bowl of soup when serving.
4. Tip: Olive oil helps the body absorb body nutrients more efficiently and supports a healthy digestive system.

Chicken Soup

Ingredients:

- 16 ounces cremini mushrooms, thinly sliced

- 4 cloves garlic, minced

- 2 stalks celery, diced

- 2 carrots, peeled and diced

- 1 onion, diced

- Kosher salt and freshly ground black pepper

- 1 pound b2less, skinless chicken breasts, cut into 1-inch chunks

- 2 tablespoons olive oil, divided

- 2 tablespoons chopped fresh parsley leaves

- Juice of 1 lemon

- 1-15 ounce can cannellini beans, drained and rinsed

- 1 bunch kale, stems removes and leaves chopped

- 1 sprig rosemary

- 2 bay leaves

- 8 cups chicken stock

- ½ teaspoon dried oregano

- ½ teaspoon dried thyme

Directions:

1. Heat a tablespoon of olive oil in a large stockpot over medium heat.

2. Season chicken with salt and pepper and add it to the stockpot. Cook until golden brown and set aside.

3. Add the remaining tablespoon of oil to the
    stockpot. Add onion, carrots, and celery. Cook
    as you stir occasionally, until tender.
4. Add garlic and mushroom and cook while
    stirring occasionally, until tender and
    browned. Stir in thyme and oregano and cook
    until fragrant.
5. Then whisk in the bay leaves as well as the
    chicken stock then bring it to a boil. Stir in
    rosemary and chicken, reduce the heat, and
    simmer until chicken is tender.
6. Stir in kale and cannellini beans, and cook
    until the kale has wilted. Stir in lemon juice
    and parsley; season with salt and pepper to
    taste.
7. Serve immediately.

Coconut-Almond Dipping Sauce

Ingredients:

- 1 tbsp. lime juice

- 1 tsp. coconut aminos

- 1 tsp. white miso paste

- 2 tbsp. coconut milk

- 1 tbsp. almond butter

- Fresh ginger, to taste

Directions:

1. Mix all the sauce Ingredients: using a blender.

2. Blend until the mixture is smooth and creamy.

3. Adjust to the consistency that you prefer by adding coconut milk.

Curry Raw Dressing

Ingredients:

- 1 tbsp. agave

- 2 tsp. sweet yellow curry powder

- 1/2 tsp. nama shoyu

- 1/2 cup cashews, soaked for at least 6 hours and drained

- 1/2 cup almond milk

- Himalayan salt, to taste

Directions:

1. In a blender, blend the dressing Ingredients: together until mixture becomes smooth.

Good Ol' Raw Guacamole

Ingredients:

- 1 tomato, diced

- Juice from 1 lime

- 1/2 small pepper, finely diced

- 2 avocados, mashed

- 1 medium purple onion, diced

- Pinch of Celtic sea salt

Directions:

1. In a bowl, combine everything together.

Red Wine Vinaigrette

Ingredients:

- 1 tbsp. lemon juice

- 1 tsp. agave nectar

- 1/2 tsp. salt

- 1/4 cup olive oil

- 2 tbsp. red wine vinegar

- Pepper, freshly ground

Directions:

1. Pour the vinegar in a food processor along with the lemon juice, agave, salt and pepper.
2. While the motor in the food processor is still running, slowly add in the olive oil.

3. Continue mixing until the mixture is well
    incorporated.

4. Drizzle the vinaigrette all over the salad and
    mix.

Wild H2y And Sesame Sauce

Ingredients:

- 1 tbsp. lemon juice

- 1 tsp. agave nectar

- 1/2 tsp. salt

- 1/4 cup olive oil

- 2 tbsp. red wine vinegar

- Pepper, freshly ground

Directions:

1. Pour the vinegar in a food processor along with the lemon juice, agave, salt and pepper.
2. While the motor in the food processor is still running, slowly add in the olive oil.

3. Continue mixing until the mixture is well
    incorporated.

Tagine Stew

Ingredients:

- 1 teaspoon ground coriander

- 1 teaspoon ground paprika

- 1/2 teaspoon ground cinnamon

- 1/4 teaspoon ground ginger

- 1/4 teaspoon saffron threads (optional)

- 1 can (15 oz) chickpeas, drained and rinsed

- 1 cup chicken broth

- 1 cup mixed vegetables (carrots, bell peppers, zucchini)

- 1/2 cup dried apricots, chopped

- 4 chicken thighs (or any preferred cut of chicken)

- 2 tablespoons olive oil

- 1 large onion, chopped

- 3 cloves garlic, minced

- 1 teaspoon ground cumin

- Salt and freshly ground black pepper to taste

- Fresh cilantro or parsley for garnish

Directions:

1. Season the chicken pieces with salt and freshly ground black pepper.
2. Heat the olive oil in a large, heavy-bottomed pot or Dutch oven over medium-high heat. Sear the chicken until it develops a golden-

brown crust on both sides. Remove the
chicken and set it aside.

3. In the same pot, add the chopped onion and
    sauté for a few minutes until softened. Add
    the minced garlic and continue to sauté for
    another minute until fragrant.

4. Stir in the ground cumin, coriander, paprika,
    cinnamon, ginger, and saffron (if using). Cook
    the spices for a minute or 3 to release their
    flavors.

5. Return the seared chicken to the pot. Add
    chickpeas, chicken broth, mixed vegetables,
    and dried apricots.

6. Bring the mixture to a boil. Then, reduce the
    heat to low, cover the pot, and let the tagine
    simmer for about 45 minutes to 1 hour, or
    until the chicken is tender and the flavors
    meld together.

7. Taste the tagine and adjust the seasoning with more salt and pepper if needed.

8. Garnish the tagine with fresh cilantro or parsley and serve it hot. Traditionally, tagine is often served with couscous or crusty bread.

9. Tagine stew is a delightful and aromatic dish that showcases the richness of North African cuisine. While this recipe features chicken, tagine can be prepared with various proteins and a wide array of vegetables and spices. Enjoy the wonderful flavors and cultural heritage that tagine brings to your table.

Tomato Basil Soup

Ingredients:

- 2 cans (28 oz each) whole tomatoes or crushed tomatoes

- 1 cup vegetable or chicken broth

- 1/4 cup fresh basil leaves, chopped

- Salt and freshly ground black pepper, to taste

- 2 tablespoons olive oil

- 1 large onion, chopped

- 3 cloves garlic, minced

- 1/2 cup heavy cream (optional, for a creamier version)

Directions:

1. In a large pot, heat the olive oil over medium heat. Add the chopped onion and sauté until it becomes translucent, about 5 minutes.
2. Stir in the minced garlic and cook for an additional 30 seconds until fragrant.
3. Add the canned tomatoes, including their juice, to the pot. If using whole tomatoes, break them up with a wooden spoon.
4. Stir in the vegetable or chicken broth, along with salt and freshly ground black pepper.
5. Allow the soup to simmer for about 15-20 minutes, letting the flavors meld. If desired, you can use an immersion blender to puree the soup until smooth.
6. Alternatively, transfer the soup to a blender in batches, blend until smooth, and return it to the pot.

7. Stir in the chopped fresh basil leaves. The basil will infuse the soup with its aromatic flavor.

8. Taste the soup and adjust the seasoning with more salt and pepper, if needed. If you prefer a creamier soup, you can add the heavy cream at this point.

9. Let the soup simmer for an additional 5-10 minutes to allow the basil's flavor to further develop.

10. Ladle the Tomato Basil Soup into bowls, garnish with additional fresh basil leaves if desired, and serve hot. You can also serve it with a side of crusty bread or a grilled cheese sandwich for a classic combination.

11. This Tomato Basil Soup is a wonderful embodiment of Mediterranean cuisine, showcasing the simplicity and health benefits of fresh Ingredients:.

12. Whether served on its own or as part of a larger meal, it's a comforting and satisfying dish that's perfect for any season. Enjoy the rich flavors and nourishment of this classic soup.

Vegetable Chicken Garlic Soup

Ingredients:

- ½ cup of fresh cream

- 2 tbsp corn starch

- Juice of 1 lemon

- 1 tsp salt

- 1/8 teaspoon of turmeric powder

- ¼ teaspoon of whole spice mix - cloves, cardamom

- 1 tsp freshly ground pepper

- 1 liter of water

- 2 large cups of vegetable fiber after juicing

- 1 cup of chicken wings

- 1 handful of freshly cut mint leaves

- 1 small onion cut into cubes

- 1 tablespoon of diced cloves of garlic

- 2 tablespoons of ghee

- 1 tablespoon of butter for garnish

Directions:

1. Fry the chicken in ghee with the onion, turmeric and whole herbs for about 10 minutes.

2. Add the vegetable fiber (taken after squeezing vegetables), mint leaves, cornstarch, cream, milk to water and simmer for another 20 minutes until the chicken turns soft and juicy.

3. Season with pepper, lemon juice and a dash of butter.

Lentils Turmeric Pineapple Soup

Ingredients:

- 1 cup of fresh coconut milk

- 1 tbsp corn starch

- Juice of 1 lemon

- 1 teaspoon of kosher salt

- 1 tsp freshly ground pepper

- 4 cups of water

- 1 tbsp butter for garnish

- 1 cup of pineapple peeled and diced

- 1 cup pre-soaked mix of green, yellow, and red lentils

- 1 handful of freshly chopped mint / coriander leaves

- 1 small onion cut into cubes

- 1 tbsp olive oil

Directions:

1. Soak the lentils in pre-cooked 2 cups of water for 20 minutes and mash with pineapple cubes, olive oil, onion and mint / cilantro leaves.
2. Add the pureed soup mix to the remaining water and coconut milk, starch and salt.
3. Let it simmer for 20 minutes.
4. Season it with pepper, lemon juice and butter and serve piping hot.

Fruit Vegetable Soup

Ingredients:

- 1 handful of freshly chopped mint / coriander leaves

- 1 small onion cut into cubes

- 1 tablespoon of freshly chopped ginger garlic

- 1 tbsp olive oil

- 2 cups of fresh almond milk

- Juice of 1 lemon

- 1 teaspoon of Himalayan sea salt

- 1 tsp peppercorns

- 2 cups of water

- 1 cube of cheese for garnish

- 1 cup of fresh peas

- 1 cup of carrots peeled and diced

- 2 tomatoes

- 1 sweet potato peeled and grated

- 1 apple seeded and cut

- 1 apricot seeds removed and cut

- 1 cup of raisins as a topping

Directions:

1. Mix the fruits and vegetables in a blender into a smooth paste.

2. Fry the onion and ginger garlic paste in olive oil until translucent.

3. Add the vegetable and fruit mixture to almond milk, water and herbs and let it cook for 20 minutes on low heat.

4. Cover it with grated cheese, mint / cilantro
    leaves and raisins.

Mango Cucumber Summer Soup

Ingredients:

- ½ cup of goat cheese

- 1 small onion cut into cubes

- 1 teaspoon freshly chopped ginger garlic

- 1 tbsp clarified butter

- 1 cup of milk

- 2 cups of water

- 2 mangoes peeled, seeded and diced

- 2 large cucumbers peeled and diced

- 2 zucchini peeled and sliced

- Handful of fresh mint leaves.

Directions:

1. Fry the onion and ginger garlic paste with clarified butter until flavorful.
2. Add water and milk to the sauté along with the cheese, cucumber and zucchini and cook over medium heat for 15 minutes.
3. Blend the prepared concoction in the blender to get a smooth paste.
4. Pour the soup into bowls and cover with mango cubes and a few fresh mint leaves.

Tomato Basil Red Pepper Soup

Ingredients:

- 1 small onion cut into cubes

- 1 teaspoon freshly chopped ginger garlic

- 1 tablespoon of ghee

- 1 cup of milk

- 2 cups of water

- 1/2 teaspoon of salt

- 6 large tomatoes cut into cubes

- 2 peppers cut into cubes

- 1/2 cup freshly chopped basil leaves

- ½ cup of cream

- 1/2 teaspoon freshly ground pepper

Directions:

1. Fry the onion with ghee until it becomes flavorful. Add the ginger garlic paste and cook for 5 minutes.
2. Add the tomatoes, paprika, salt, pepper, milk and water and cook for 20 minutes over medium heat.
3. Add the cream and blend the soup mix in 3 parts in the blender to get an even, smooth paste.
4. Cook for another 5 minutes.
5. Cover with fresh basil leaves and serve immediately.

Egg Noodle Black Pepper Soup

Ingredients:

- 1/4 cup of cream

- 1 small onion cut into cubes

- 1 teaspoon freshly chopped ginger garlic

- 1 tbsp olive oil

- 2 cups of vegetable stock or water

- 1/2 teaspoon of salt

- 2 large eggs from the farm

- 1 cup of noodles

- 1/2 cup freshly chopped basil leaves

- 1/2 teaspoon freshly ground pepper

Directions:

1. In a stockpot, sauté the onions, finely chopped ginger garlic with olive oil until the aroma rises for 5 minutes.
2. Pour in the vegetable stock or water, basil leaves and herbs and let it come to a boil.
3. Beat the eggs with a fork or an egg beater and keep them separately.
4. Add the noodles and in a single stem, pour the beaten eggs into the boiling soup mix to form strings.
5. Cook on high heat for up to 10 minutes. The noodles would have gotten softer by then.
6. Serve immediately with a drizzle of cream on top and enjoy.

Cherry Tomato Mixed Veg Minestr2 Soup

Ingredients:

- 1 small onion cut into cubes

- 1 teaspoon freshly diced garlic

- 1 tbsp fresh cilantro

- Peel of 1 lemon and juice

- 1 tbsp olive oil

- 4 cups of vegetable stock or water

- ½ teaspoon of salt

- 250 grams of cherry tomatoes

- 250 grams of mixed vegetables (potatoes, carrots, beans) cut into small pieces

- 100 grams of spaghetti (broken into medium / short length)

- ½ tsp freshly ground pepper

Directions:

1. In a stockpot add olive oil and sauté the onions and diced garlic for 5 minutes.
2. Add the chopped vegetables and cook for another 10 minutes to soften them.
3. Pour in the vegetable stock and add the cherry tomatoes and lemon zest - cook for another 10 minutes.
4. Add spaghetti and cook for another 10 minutes over medium heat.
5. Serve immediately with a spoonful of fresh cream topped with a little coriander leaves.
6. Sprinkle with the herbs and lemon juice to taste and enjoy.

Lentil Turmeric Pineapple Soup

Ingredients:

- 1 tbsp olive oil

- 1 cup fresh coconut milk

- 1 tbsp corn starch

- Juice of 1 lemon

- 1 tsp kosher salt

- 1 tsp freshly ground pepper

- 4 cups water

- 1 cup of pineapple peeled and cubed

- 1 cup pre-soaked mix of green, yellow and red lentils

- 1 handful freshly cut mint/cilantro leaves

- 1 small onion diced

- 1 tbsp butter for garnish

Directions:

1. Soak the lentils for 20 minutes in par boiled 2 cups of water and puree them with pineapple cubes, olive oil, onion and mint/cilantro leaves.

2. Add the pureed soup mix to the remaining water and coconut milk, starch and salt. Allow it to simmer for 20 minutes.

3. Spice it with pepper, juice of lemon and butter before serving it piping hot.

Fruit Vegetable Soup

Ingredients:

- 1 small onion diced

- 1 tbsp freshly minced ginger garllc

- 1 tbsp olive oil

- 2 cups fresh almond milk

- Juice of 1 lemon

- 1 tsp Himalayan sea salt

- 1 tsp peppercorns

- 2 cups water

- 1 cube cheese for garnish

- 1 cup fresh peas

- 1 cup carrots peeled and diced

- 2 tomatoes

- 1 sweet potato peeled and grated

- 1 apple deseeded and cut

- 1 apricot deseeded and cut

- 1 handful freshly cut mint/cilantro leaves

- 1 cup raisins for topping

Directions:

1. Blend the fruits and vegetables in a blender to form a smooth paste.
2. Sauté the onions and ginger garlic paste in olive oil till translucent.
3. Add the vegetable and fruit blend to almond milk, water and spices and let it boil on slow heat for 20 minutes.

4. Top it with grated cheese, mint/cilantro

    leaves and raisins.

Mango Cucumber Summer Soup

Ingredients:

- ½ cup goat cheese

- 1 small onion diced

- 1 tsp freshly minced ginger garlic

- 1 tbsp clarified butter

- 1 cup milk

- 2 cups water

- 2 mangoes peeled deseeded and cubed

- 2 large cucumber peeled and diced

- 2 zucchini peeled and sliced

- Handful of fresh mint leaves.

Directions:

1. Sauté the onion and ginger garlic paste with clarified butter till it becomes flavorful.
2. Add water and milk to the sauté along with the cheese, cucumber and zucchini and let it boil on medium flame for 15 minutes.
3. Blend the prepared concoction in the blender to get a smooth paste.
4. Pour the soup into bowls and top them with mango cubes and a couple of fresh mint leaves.

Tomato Basil Red Pepper Soup

Ingredients:

- ½ cup cream

- 1 small onion diced

- 1 tsp freshly minced ginger garlic

- 1 tbsp ghee

- 1 cup milk

- 2 cups water

- 1/2 tsp salt

- 6 large tomatoes cut in cubes

- 2 bell peppers diced

- 1/2 cup freshly chopped basil leaves

- 1/2 tsp freshly ground pepper

Directions:

1. Sauté the onions with ghee till it becomes flavorful. Add in the ginger garlic paste and saute for 5 minutes.
2. Drop in the tomatoes, bell peppers, salt, pepper, milk and water and let it boil on medium flame for 20 minutes.
3. Add the cream and blend the soup mix in 3 parts in the blender to get a uniform smooth paste. Boil for another 5 minutes.
4. Top it with fresh basil leaves and serve immediately.

Low Fodmap Summer Garden Vegetable Soup

INGREDIENTS:

- 2 medium carrots, peeled and cut into bite-sized pieces on the diagonal

- 12 ounces (340 g) plum tomatoes, cored and chopped

- 6 ounces (170 g) green beans, ends trimmed, cut into thirds

- 1 medium zucchini, ends trimmed away, cut into quarters lengthwise, then cut into bit-sized chunks

- 1 cup (164 g) yellow corn kernels, fresh off the cob

- 1/2 large fennel bulb, stalks and fronds discarded, cut into 1/2-inch (12 mm) wide slices

- 2 ounces (55 g) kale, tough stems removed, torn into large bite-sized pieces

- 3 ounce (85 g) piece of rind of Parmesan cheese (omit if vegan)

- Kosher salt

- 1/4 cup (60 ml) olive oil

- 2 whole garlic cloves, peeled

- 1 cup (48 g) finely sliced leeks, green parts only

- 1/4 cup (16 g) finely chopped scallions, green parts only

- 8 cups (2 L) Low FODMAP Vegetable Broth, homemade or purchased

- 1 pound (455 g) red potatoes, scrubbed and cut into large bite-sized pieces

- Freshly ground black pepper

- Low FODMAP Basil Pesto, optional

DIRECTIONS:

1. Heat oil in a 5-quart (4.7 L) Dutch oven or similar size stockpot over low-medium heat.
2. Add garlic cloves and sauté for a minute or two until garlic is softened, but not browned.
3. Remove all of the pieces of garlic; this is very important to keep the recipe low FODMAP.
4. Once all of the garlic pieces are removed add leek and scallion greens and sauté for about 3

minutes or until softened but do not let them brown.

5. Add broth, potatoes and carrots and bring to a simmer. Cover and simmer for about 10 to 15 minutes or until potatoes and carrots are just tender when pierced with a knife.

6. Add tomatoes, beans, zucchini, corn, fennel, kale and cheese rind and simmer for about 20 to 25 minutes or until vegetables are cooked but still retain some vibrancy of color.

7. Season to taste with salt and pepper, going light on the salt if you plan on using the pesto.

8. Soup is ready to serve. Ladle into bowls and stir about 2 teaspoons of Basil Pesto into each serving, if desired.

9. Soup can be refrigerated in airtight containers for up to 4 days or frozen for 1 month.

Low Fodmap Pho Bo

INGREDIENTS:

Toppings:

- Mint

- Thai basil

- Red Thai chiles thinly sliced

Soup:

- 4 whole cloves

- 2 whole star anise

- 1, 3-inch (7.5 cm) cinnamon stick

- 1 teaspoon coriander seed

- 1 teaspoon fennel seed

- 2 tablespoons fish sauce or to taste

- 1 teaspoon sugar, optional, or to taste

- 4 cups (about ¾ pound; 320 g) mung bean sprouts

- 1/3 pound (153 g) eye of round, London broil, filet mignon or rib eye

- 2 large leeks, with a good amount of green parts attached

- 2- inch (5 cm) piece fresh ginger, unpeeled

- 8 cups (2 L) Beef Stock, homemade or low FODMAP purchased equivalent

- 1 pound (455 g) banh pho rice noodles, we like 1/8-inch or 1/4-inch wide (3mm to 6 mm)

- 1/2 cup (36 g) sliced scallions, green parts only

- 1/4 cup (8 g) cilantro leaves

- Lime wedges

DIRECTIONS:

1. Prepare Toppings: Prepare toppings so that they are ready to serve. We like to arrange the mint, Thai basil and sliced chiles on a platter, leaving room for some bean sprouts. Set aside.

2. Freeze the Meat: Place the meat in the freezer for about 20 minutes or just until ice crystals begin to form. This will allow you to cut it super thin. Meanwhile, proceed with the other prep.

3. Char the Leeks and Ginger: You will note that the recipe calls for whole leeks, whereas you probably know by now that only the green parts are low FODMAP. We are going to char the leek greens and it is just easier to maneuver using the whole leek; please follow

the Directions: carefully. Char the leek greens and the ginger by placing directly over a gas flame. If you do not have gas, place on a rack set on a baking sheet pan under the broiler. In either case, rotate the leeks and ginger several times with tongs so that they get a good black char all the way around. Cool. Use your fingers and a small paring knife to remove all of the black charred parts. Roughly chop the leek greens and the ginger and add to a large pot. It is imperative to only use the green parts of the leek; discard the rest of the leek stalks.

4. Create the Flavored Stock: Add Beef Stock to the pot along with the cloves, star anise, cinnamon stick, coriander and fennel, cover and simmer over low heat for about 1 hour.

5. Soak the Noodles: Place noodles in a large, deep bowl and cover with hot for about 15

minutes or until pliable. Meanwhile continue with other prep.

6. Slice the Meat: While the noodles are soaking and stock is simmering, remove beef from freezer and cut against the grain as thinly as possible but definitely no thicker than 1/4-inch. The dimensions should be large bite-sized pieces. Set aside; beef should be room temperature when you assemble the Pho.

7. Strain and Season the stock: Taste the stock; it should be well flavored. Strain the stock, discarding solids. Return stock to pot. Taste and season to taste with fish sauce and optional sugar, if using. Keep stock hot over low heat.

8. Blanch Bean Sprouts and Cook Noodles: Bring a large pot of water to a boil. Blanch bean sprouts for about 10 to 15 seconds and remove them with a strainer. Shake them dry

and place a mound on the Toppings platter; set the majority of them aside to be used in assembly. Add noodles to boiling water and cook just until al dente, which will only take a few minutes. Drain and set aside.

9. Assemble Pho: Warm deep soup bowls with very hot water and dry. Place noodles in each bowl, then top with several slices of raw beef, fanned out to expose maximum surface area. Add a small mound of reserved bean sprouts to the side. Bring stock to a boil and ladle over the meat and sprouts; the heat will cook the meat. Quickly garnish with sliced scallions, cilantro and lime wedges and serve immediately. Encourage diners to add toppings of their choice and dig in!

INGREDIENTS:

- 1 medium celery stalk, cut into 2-inch (5 cm) pieces

- 2 tablespoons tomato paste

- 1 tablespoon black peppercorns

- 1 tablespoon low-sodium soy sauce, use gluten-free if following a gluten-free diet

- 2 teaspoons kosher salt

- 1/2 bunch fresh flat leaf parsley, roughly torn

- 4 medium sprigs fresh thyme

- 2 bay leaves

- 14 cups water

- 1/4 cup (60 ml) of EITHER Low FODMAP
  Garlic-Infused Oil or Onion-Infused Oil, made
  with vegetable oil or purchased equivalent

- 4 pounds (1.8 kg) of beef bones, such as a
  combination of meaty neck bones, knuckle
  bones, oxtail and marrow bones, cut into 2-
  inch (5 cm) thick pieces by the butcher

- 3 cups (145 g) roughly chopped leeks, green
  parts only

- 2 medium carrots, scrubbed and cut into 2-
  inch (5 cm) pieces

- 2 medium (225 g) parsnips, scrubbed and cut
  into 2-inch (5 cm) pieces

- Cheesecloth

DIRECTIONS:

1. Position rack in center of oven. Preheat oven to 450°F/230°C. Have a heavy, rimmed sheet pan at hand.

2. Heat oil over medium heat in a large 8 to 10 quart (7.5 L to 9.5 L) heavy stockpot.

3. Add the meaty bones and begin to brown them in the oil for about 3 minutes or until you get all the meaty bone surfaces infused with the flavorful oil.

4. Scatter the leeks all over the sheet pan. Don't wash the stockpot, as you will be returning to it shortly.

5. Transfer the browned bones to the sheet pan on top of the leeks. Roast for 20 minutes, stir the leeks and bones around and roast for 20 to 25 more minutes or until the bones are well browned. Don't worry if the leeks look a little charred.

6. Scrape everything from the sheet pan, juices and all, into the waiting stockpot.

7. Add carrots, parsnips, celery, tomato paste, peppercorns, soy sauce, salt, parsley, thyme and bay leaves to pot.

8. Add the 14 cups of water; It should cover the solids. Add more water if it doesn't just to cover all of the ingredients by about an inch (2.5 cm).

9. Bring stock to a very low simmer. Cover but leave lid slightly ajar and adjust heat so that the stock can simmer for an extended period of time. You want the surface just rippling.

10. Check from time to time and skim any froth that might rise to the surface and discard.

11. Also check water levels; add water as needed to keep solids submerged.

12. Gently simmer for at least 12 hours; we let ours simmer overnight for 24 hours, but use

your judgment about whether you feel

comfortable with this.

Coconut-Mangosteen Soup

Ingredients:

- 2 tsp Ghee (clarified butter)

- ¼ tsp CumIn Seeds

- ¼ tsp Asafetida

- 1 tbsp Coriander leaves

- ¼ tsp green Chili Paste

- 1 tsp Sugar

- 2 cup Coconut Milk

- 3-4 Mangosteens (you can use mangosteen syrup) (Mangosteen is also called 'fish tamarind')

- Salt to taste

Directions:

1. Wash the mangosteens and mash them in ½ a cup of water to create a pulpy, pink syrup.
2. Add this pulpy syrup to coconut milk and mix well.
3. Also add sugar, salt, green chili paste and coriander leaves to this mixture and mix well.
4. Heat the Ghee in a pan.
5. Once the Ghee is hot, add the cumin seeds and asafetida. To the pan.
6. Once the cumin starts crackling, add the contents of the pan to the soup mixture and mix it well.
7. Then heat it over a medium flame. (only heat it, don't bring it to a boil)

Potato Soup

Ingredients:

- 2 tsp Butter

- 3 tbsp Spring Onions (finely chopped)

- ¼ tsp Black Pepper Powder

- 2 medium sized Potatoes

- 1 cup Coconut Milk

- Salt to taste

Directions:

1. Peel off the skin of the Potatoes and cut them into thin slices.

2. Heat the butter in a pot. When it melts add the spring onions and stir for a minute. Then add the potato slices and stir them for a while.

3. Pour in 2-3 cups of water into the pot and let it simmer till the potato slices are cooked perfectly.

4. Then make a paste of the contents of the pot using a blender and set this paste aside.

5. Now add salt and black pepper powder to the coconut milk followed by the potato=spring onion paste and bring it to a boil over a medium heat.

6. Garnish with chopped coriander leaves and serve hot.

Cabbage Soup

Ingredients:

- 2 cup Coconut Milk

- ¼ tsp black Pepper Powder

- 2 tsp Ghee (Clarified Butter)

- 1 tsp Flour

- 1 cup grated Cabbage

- 1 medium sized Potato (finely diced)

- 1 medium sized Onion (finely diced)

- Salt to taste

Directions:

1. Boil potato and cabbage together in 2 cups of water till they are perfectly cooked.

2. Then use a blender to make a paste of the boiled potatoes and cabbage.

3. Heat the butter in a pot. When it melts, add the diced onions and stir till they turn light pink. Then add the flour and stir again for a while.

4. Now add the potato-cabbage paste made earlier followed by coconut milk and keep stirring continuously.

5. When it comes to a boil, add salt and black pepper powder.

6. Garnish with fresh mint leaves and serve hot.

Black-Eyed Beans Soup

Ingredients:

- 1 tbsp chopped Coriander Leaves

- ½ tsp green Chili Paste

- ½ tsp Garlic Paste

- 1 tsp Sugar

- Salt to taste

- ¼ tsp Cumin Seeds

- ¼ tsp Asafetida

- 1 cup Black-eyed Beans

- 2 cups fresh Buttermilk

- 1-2 tbsp Cooking Oil (Ghee i.e. clarified butter, Olive Oil, Avocado Oil or Coconut Oil)

Directions:

1. Roast the black-eyed beans in a pan for 3-4
    minutes.
2. Then add around 3 cups of water to the beans
    and cook the beans.
3. Once the beans are cooked, remove the water
    and store it aside. (We will not need the
    beans)
4. This bean water is the base of our soup.
5. Add the garlic paste and green chili paste to
    the bean water and mix it well.
6. Then add the buttermilk, salt and sugar to the
    bean water and mix thoroughly.
7. Now heat the mixture over a low flame. (do
    not bring it to a boil)
8. Heat the cooking oil in a pan.
9. Once the oil is hot, add the cumin seeds and
    asafetida to the pan.

10. Once the cumin starts crackling, add the
    contents of the pan to the hot soup mixture
    and mix well.

11. Garnish with fresh coriander leaves and serve
    hot.

Coconut Soup

Ingredients:

- ¼ tsp Cumin Seed Powder

- 2 tsp chopped Mint Leaves

- ½ tsp Sugar (if needed)

- Salt to taste

- ¼ tsp Asafetida

- ¼ tsp Cumin seeds

- 2 cups Coconut Milk

- 1 cup Dates

- 1 tsp Tamarind Pulp

- 2 tsp Rice Flour

- 1-2 tbsp Cooking Oil (Ghee i.e. clarified butter, Olive Oil, Avocado Oil or Coconut Oil)

Directions:

1. Keep the dates soaking in 2 cups of water for around 1 hour.
2. Then remove the seeds and make a paste of dates using a blender.
3. Add this paste to 2 cups of coconut milk followed by tamarind pulp and mix well.
4. Now add salt and cumin seed powder to the mixture. (also add sugar if needed)
5. Mix the rice flour in ½ a cup of water and then pour it in the soup mixture.
6. Then heat this mixture on a low flame and bring it to a boil.
7. While the mixture is coming to a boil, Heat the cooking oil in a pan.

8. Once the oil is hot, add the cumin seeds and asafetida to the pan.

9. Once the cumin starts crackling, add the contents of the pan to the hot soup mixture and mix well.

10. Garnish with fresh mint leaves and serve hot.

Bouillabaisse With Saffron New Potatoes

Ingredients:

FOR THE BROTH

- 500g/1lb of Onions

- 12 cloves of garlic

- 850g/2lbs of locally grown tomatoes

- Large Bunch of Bouquet Garni

- 2 bulbs of fennel

- Fresh herbs, such as basil, chervil and parsley

- About 2 kgs/4.4 lbs of assorted fish heads and fish b2s.

- 2 pack of spider crab (can be found in German supermarkets in the UK in the freezer cabinet

for around £2 or ask fishmonger for crab and
lobster shells)

- Olive oil

- 500g/1lb of Leeks

- Big squeeze of tomato purée

FOR SERVING

- 1 kg/2.2 lbs of new or Charlotte potatoes

- 2 large pinches of Saffron

- 2 kg/4.4 lbs of assorted fish, prawns and
shellfish (pollack, pouting, gurnard, salmon,
raw prawns and mussels as a guide)

- 1 French stick and garlic butter (optional)

Directions:

1. Place all the broth Ingredients: into a slow cooker and cover with boiling water. Put on a medium heat, cover and cook overnight.
2. Next morning, push the broth through a mouli (careful, it will go everywhere) or through a fine sieve. Get all the goodness out you can, so squeeze tightly.
3. Discard the debris.
4. Pour the resulting broth through a fine sieve twice, pushing with the back of a wooden spoon. You should end with a delightful smooth and fishy tomato soup. Place that into a large pressure cooker size saucepan and put on a gentle heat.
5. Parboil the peeled potatoes in the salted saffron water. They should go yellow but don't overcook them. Remove from water to prevent that.

6. Prepare your seafood. De-skin the fish, peel and de-vein the prawns but leave the tails on and chunk fish flesh into hearty pieces. Scrub mussels if using and remove any beard.

7. This is a great dinner party dish as all the above stages can be prepared in advance.

8. When you're ready to start thinking about serving, bring your tomato soup to the boil and then add your saffron potatoes. Cook for a further 5 minutes.

9. Adjust seasoning if necessary but all should be good.

10. Then add your seafood, biggest pieces first, mussels and prawns last. When the mussels open you should be ready to serve. Just test your potatoes, they should now be soft enough to eat and your fish and prawns should be d2. If any mussels refuse to open, do not serve them.

11. Half fill the bowls with soup and share the 'goodies' among the dishes and make sure every2 gets at least 2 of each different ingredient.

12. Sprinkle soup with chopped chives and if you're not on your diet, then serve with garlic crusty bread, which is simply made by diagonally slicing a French stick and spreading both sides of the slices with garlic butter (with added salt).

13. Then just put in the oven on a wire rack and bake for around 20 minutes or so, or until the bread is golden and crispy.

14. Enjoy!

Celeriac Soup

Ingredients:

- 1 chopped stick of celery.

- 1 large spoon of veggie stock powder

- Good pinch of salt

- Pinch of ground black pepper

- 1 large spoon of dried rosemary

- 2 bay leaves

- Optional: mustard, mixed herbs, salt, pepper and white wine vinegar

- 3 celeriac

- 1 chopped onion

- 2 chopped carrots

- 1 chopped leek

- Optional: 1 can of chickpeas

Directions:

1. Take 3 Celeriac and peel them by chopping away anything brown, ugly and not white.
2. Then brown 2 chopped onion to within an inch of burning. Add the cubed celeriac, along with a couple of chopped carrots, leek and celery. Add a large spoon of veggie stock powder and a good pinch of salt.
3. Add some ground black pepper, dried rosemary and 2 bay leaves and top with water.
4. Bring to the boil and cook for 30 minutes.
5. Whiz to a purée
6. Taste and adjust seasoning.

7. Purists won't add much more but you can add
   mustard, mixed herbs, salt, pepper and white
   wine vinegar to change the shape of the
   flavour.

8. Optional: If using as a lunchtime soup, then
   drain and add a can of chickpeas for extra
   energy (and nuttiness).

9. Sprinkle with chopped chives.

Root And Bean Soup

Ingredients:

- 1 cup fresh or frozen peas,

- 1 cup fresh or frozen sweetcorn

- 1 cup fresh or frozen green beans,

- 2 cups fresh or frozen broad beans

- 1 cup chopped chorizo and german or polish (garlic) sausage

- Salt, pepper

- 1 cup fresh herbs

- 1 dessert spoon of mixed dried herbs,

- 1 dessert spoon of mustard,

- 1 onion chopped,

- A few leeks, chopped

- Glug of olive oil

- Approx. 1kg/2.2 lb mix of root vegetables such
  as parsnip, carrot, celeriac, swede, turnip,
  potato

- Teaspoon each of white wine vinegar and
  sugar

Directions:

1. Chop 1 onion and a few leeks. Put in a pressure cooker sized pan, along with some olive oil. Put some colour on them.

2. While they're colouring up, peel and chop (same size cube is best) a mix of root vegetables such as parsnip, carrot, celeriac, swede, turnip, potato (in fact, anything that grows below the ground but avoid beetroot, as it will turn your soup pink!). Fry those up and put some colour on those too.

3. Then add some frozen vegetables, such as peas, sweetcorn and green beans, and a good portion of frozen broad beans. (You can use fresh peas, sweetcorn and beans if you want to).

4. Cover veg with boiling water. Chop up some Chorizo and German or Polish (garlic) sausage and add that.

5. Season with the usual suspects which include salt, pepper, fresh herbs (rosemary and thyme very good but tie those in bouquet garni if using), mixed dried herbs, mustard, white wine vinegar and sugar.

6. Enjoy!

Bacon, Sweetcorn And Chicken Soup

Ingredients:

- 1 dessert spoon of vegetable stock powder

- 2 bay leaves

- 1 teaspoon of pepper

- 1 dessert spoon of dried mixed herbs

- 1 heaped cupful of frozen sweetcorn

- Salt (if it is needed)

- A good dollop of english mustard

- 1 cup of frozen peas

- 1 cup of chopped mushrooms

- 300g /¾lb of bacon bits

- 1 chopped onion,

- 2 chopped leeks

- 1 chopped carrot

- 1 chopped stick of celery

- 2 half of a raw chicken

- 1 dessert spoon of mixed herbs,

- 1 dessert spoon of mustard

- A few sprigs of rosemary and fresh thyme, tied together, in a bouquet garni

- 1 handful of spaghetti

Directions:

1. Under a grill, brown (and I mean really brown, to a crisp) 300g of bacon bits.

2. In a [pressure cooker sized saucepan, brown some onion, leeks and add carrot and celery.

3. Add 2 half of a raw chicken and cover with water (you can always freeze the other half).

4. Add mixed herbs, mustard, a sprig of rosemary, the browned and all chopped up bacon bits, vegetable stock powder, 2 bay leaves, pepper, fresh thyme and dried mixed herbs and cover with boiling water.

5. Do NOT add salt at this stage

6. Boil and then simmer for 1 hour.

7. Then remove chicken and skim surface and remove all the gunk and fat and place into a jug. Don't worry of you get some of the good guys in the gunk, we have a plan to return them to their rightful destiny...

8. When all the fat and gunk has been removed, allow to cool in the jug and then place your

jug in your fridge overnight (or freezer if you're in a hurry).

9. Chop up the chicken flesh (removing the skin and b2s to create chicken stock which you can use in the next recipe) and return chopped flesh to the soup pot. Care should be taken when chopping the flesh to make sure no errant b2s are in there (turn the radio down and listen good).

10. Add a heaped cupful of frozen sweetcorn and adjust seasoning. (Yes, you may now also add salt if it is needed). Now is also the time to add a good dollop of English mustard.

11. Add some frozen peas and chopped mushrooms.

12. Add a handful of broken (in 3) spaghetti and cook for another 15 minutes, or until those noodles are tender.

13. Now, where did you put that jug? Fridge or freezer? Either way. when fat and gunk has solidified in the jug, spoon that out and dispose of, remembering to save any of those good guys who got caught up in the melee.

14. Return remainder of jug (minus the gunk and fat) to your soup pot.

15. Remove bouquet garni (if still around) before serving

16. **Yum!**

Bean And Barley Soup

Ingredients:

- 1 cup pearled barley

- 1 cup pinto (cooked)

- 1/3 cup tomato paste

- 1/4 teaspoon salt

- 1/2 teaspoon pepper

- 1/4 teaspoon celery salt

- 1/2 teaspoon basil

- 1/2 teaspoon oregano

- 1/2 large onion (diced)

- 2-3 cloves garlic (minced)

- 2 tablespoons of oil

- 2 ribs celery (diced)

- 2 medium-sized carrots (diced)

- 2 any

  vegetables (1/2 cup each)

- 8 cups water

- 1/2 teaspoon thyme

1 teaspoon onion powder

2 large bay leaves

Directions:

1. In a large soup pot, sautee the onions, and garlic in oil for a minute or 3, then add the celery, carrots and any other vegetables for 3-5 minutes.

2. Add vegetable broth or water and all other
    remaining Ingredients: and bring to a simmer.
    Once your soup is simmering, reduce the heat
    to medium-low and cover your pot.

3. Allow to simmer for at least thirty minutes
    and up to 2 hour, stirring occasionally, until
    barley is soft and some what fluffy.

4. Remove the bay leaves before serving your
    soup. Taste, add more spices or salt and
    pepper to taste and enjoy.

Mayan Maize Soup

Ingredients:

- 2 tablespoons margarine

- 8 ounces cream cheese

- 1 lb Mexican cheese (cubed)

- 17 ounces cream style corn

- 1/2 cup green pepper(chopped)

- 1/4 cup onion (chopped)

- 1 1/2 cups milk

Directions:

1. Saute green peppers and onions in margarine.
2. Add cream cheese and stir until melted. Add cheese, milk and corn.

3. Heat until melted, stirring occasionally.

4. Garnish with thin strips of red pepper and
    cilantro.

Egg Dope Soup

Ingredients:

- 2 tablespoons cold water

- 1 tablespoon cornstarch

- 1 egg

- 1 scallion (finely chopped)

- 3 cups chicken broth

- 1/2 teaspoon salt

Directions:

1. Bring chicken broth to a boil in soup pot.
2. Add 1/2 teaspoon salt & mix.
3. Combine water and cornstarch stir into boiling broth.

4. Stir a small amount of hot broth into slightly
    beaten egg. Add egg mixture into hot broth
    slowly, stirring all the time. Cook until clear
    and slightly thickened, stirring constantly.
5. Garnish with scallion.

Priyapita Soup

Ingredients:

- 1/4 cup fresh basil(chopped)

- 1/2 cup cornmeal

- 6 cans beef broth

- 10 ounces green chili salsa

- 1 onion(chopped)

- 1 can tomatoes(diced)

- 1/2 teaspoon dried basil

- 1/2 teaspoon dried oregano

- 1/4 teaspoon black pepper (ground)

- 1 lb ground chuck

- 1/4 lb pork sausage

- 1 onion(chopped)

- 1 egg(beaten)

- 1/2 teaspoon salt

- 1/4 teaspoon black pepper (ground)

- 1/4 teaspoon garlic powder

- 1/4 cup milk

- 1/2 cup rice

Directions:

1. Mix together beef broth, salsa, 1 onion, tomatoes, dried basil, oregano, and 1/4 teaspoon pepper.

2. Eliminate the salt in the meatballs and use 5 cans broth plus 2 quart water. Bring to a boil

and simmer 20 minutes.

Combine ground chuck, sausage, 1 onion, egg, salt, 1/4 teas poon pepper, garlic powder, milk, fresh basil, and cornmeal, and mix well.

3. Form into tiny, bite-size meatballs.
4. Add meatballs and rice to broth.
5. Simmer, covered, very slowly for 1 to 1 1/2 hours.

Chicken Detox Soup

Ingredients:

- 2 1/2 cups sliced carrots

- 2 cups chopped celery

- 1 1/2 cups frozen peas

- 1/4 cup chopped parsley

- 3 tablespoons fresh ginger, shredded or grated

- 4 garlic cloves minced

- 2 tablespoons olive oil

- 1 tablespoon apple cider vinegar

- 1/4 - 1/2 teaspoon crushed red pepper

- 1/4 teaspoon ground turmeric

- 1 1/2 pounds boneless skinless chicken breast

- 2 quarts chicken broth

- 1 large onion, peeled and chopped

- 3 cups broccoli florets

- Salt and pepper

Directions:

1. Set a large sauce pot over medium heat. Add the olive oil, chopped onions, celery, ginger, and garlic.

2. Saute for 5-6 minutes to soften. Then add the raw chicken breasts, broth, carrots, apple cider vinegar, crushed red pepper, turmeric and 1 teaspoon sea salt.

3. Bring to a boil, lower the heat, and simmer for 20+ minutes, until the chicken breasts are cooked through. Then remove the chicken with tongs and set them on a cutting board to cool.

4. Add the broccoli, peas, and parsley to the pot. Continue to simmer to soften the broccoli.

5. Meanwhile, shred the chicken breasts with 3 forks, and stir it back into the soup. Once the broccoli is tender, taste, then salt and pepper as needed. Serve warm.

Rustic Vegetable Soup

Ingredients:

- 1 tbsp chopped fresh thyme

- 1 leek, finely sliced

- 175g bite-sized cauliflower florets

- 1 courgette, chopped

- 3 garlic cloves, finely chopped

- ½ large Savoy cabbage, stalks removed and leaves chopped

- 1 tbsp basil, chopped

- 1 tbsp rapeseed oil

- 1 large onion, chopped

- 2 carrots, chopped

- 2 celery sticks, chopped

- 50g dried red lentils

- 1½ l boiling vegetable bouillon (we used Marigold)

- 2 tbsp tomato purée

Directions:

1. Heat the oil in a large pan with a lid.
2. Add the onion, carrots and celery and fry for 10 mins, stirring from time to time until they are starting to colour a little around the edges.
3. Stir in the lentils and cook for 1 min more.
4. Pour in the hot bouillon, add the tomato purée and thyme and stir well. Add the leek, cauliflower, courgette, and garlic, bring to the

boil, then cover and leave to simmer for 15 mins.

5. Add the cabbage and basil and cook for 5 mins more until the veg is just tender. Season with pepper, ladle into bowls and serve.

6. Will keep in the fridge for a couple of days. Freezes well. Thaw, then reheat in a pan until piping hot.

B2 Broth

Ingredients:

- Zest and juice 1 lemon

- 2 bay leaves

- 1-2 red chillies , halved, deseeded and sliced

- 1 tsp ground coriander

- ½ tsp ground cumin

- Small pack coriander , stems and leaves chopped and separated

- 1 large garlic clove , finely grated

- 1 meaty chicken carcass, plus any jellified roasting juices from it, skin and fat discarded

- 1 large onion , halved and sliced

- Optional topping

- 250g pouch wholegrain basmati rice

Directions:

1. Break the chicken carcass into a large pan and add the onion, 1.5 litres of water, the lemon juice and bay leaves.

2. Cover and simmer for 40 mins. Remove from the heat and allow to cool slightly, to make things a bit easier to handle.

3. Place a colander over a bowl and scoop out all the bones into the colander. Pick through them, stripping off the chicken and returning it with any onion as you work your way down the pile of b2s.

4. Return any broth from the bowl to the pan – and any jellified roasting juices – along with

the chilli, ground coriander, cumin, coriander
stems, lemon zest and garlic.

5. Cook for a few mins until just bubbling – don't
overboil as you will spoil the delicate flavours.
Taste, and season only if you need to.

6. Meanwhile, heat the rice following pack
instructions, then toss with the coriander
leaves. Ladle the broth into bowls and top
with the rice.

9 788879 509616